YOU ARE CALLED
To Him and For Him

WAYNE HANCOCK

Copyright © 2015 by Wayne Hancock

You Are Called
To Him and For Him
by Wayne Hancock

Printed in the United States of America.

ISBN 9781498443012

All rights reserved solely by the author. The author guarantees all contents are original and do not infringe upon the legal rights of any other person or work. No part of this book may be reproduced in any form without the permission of the author. The views expressed in this book are not necessarily those of the publisher.

Unless otherwise indicated, Scripture quotations taken from the New King James Version (NKJV). Copyright © 1982 by Thomas Nelson, Inc. Used by permission. All rights reserved.

Scripture quotations taken from the New Living Translation (NLT). Copyright © 1996, 2004, 2007 by Tyndale House Foundation. Used by permission. All rights reserved.

Scripture quotations taken from The Message (MSG). Copyright © 1993, 1994, 1995, 1996, 2000, 2001, 2002. Used by permission of NavPress Publishing Group. Used by permission. All rights reserved.

Scripture quotations taken from the King James Version (KJV) – public domain.

Scripture quotations taken from the New English Translation (NET Bible). Copyright ©1996-2006 by Biblical Studies Press, L.L.C. Used by permission. All rights reserved.

Scripture quotations marked TLB are taken from The Living Bible. Copyright © 1971 by Tyndale House Publishers, Inc., Wheaton, Illinois.

Scripture quotations marked YLT are taken from the Young's Literal Translation.

Scripture.quotations taken from the Amplified Bible (AMP). Copyright © 1954, 1958, 1962, 1964, 1965, 1987 by The Lockman Foundation. Used by permission. All rights reserved.

www.xulonpress.com

What others are saying about
You Are Called to Him and for Him

Pastor Wayne is a long-time friend and co-laborer in the Lord. I have witnessed his faithfulness to his calling as a pastor, and his excellence as a family man. He lives his commitment to the Word of God.

His book, *You Are Called to Him and for Him*, is so timely in this hour when clarity and understanding of who we are is needed like never before in the Body of Christ. God's plan for you is that He be first in your life. How great is the depth of your connection to Him? Your call is significant and important to God and His body. Are you in position?

Wayne has written knowledgeably and extensively about the call of God—what it is and what it is not. He shares what he's learned and how that understanding has affected his life, his family and his church.

I highly recommend this book. It's impactful and promotes growth and maturity as you pursue your own personal calling in Christ Jesus. It's a door to victorious living as we face the challenges of these last days.

Dr. Jerry Savelle
Jerry Savelle Ministries International
www.jsmi.org

The prophet Isaiah was given the supernatural privilege of hearing and recording a conversation within the Triune Godhead taking place in the very throne room of Heaven. The account, given in the book of Isaiah chapter 6, verse 8 (NKJV) reads: *"Also I heard the voice of the Lord, saying: 'Whom shall I send, And who will go for Us?' Then I said, 'Here am I! Send me.'"*

The furtherance of this question specifically uses the term "Us" as the motivation for the mission of the one who would accept such a divine calling. History, both past and present, has recorded the legacy of men and women who have heard His sovereign voice calling to serve, and launched forth with "good ideas," yet not "God's ideas or ideals."

To heed that call for only notoriety or personal gain produces "charisma without character," as well as "passion without power." The beaches of time are littered with the wreckage of those who never really understood the call or the heart of the very One who was calling.

Pastor Wayne has been given, and in this book, offers insights into the true meaning of being "called" by God. Readers will have their own understanding broadened and begin to realize that being "called" places the Body of Christ on an even plain, not overshadowed by the offices of the five-fold ministry gifts. The reader will also see that this does not lessen the placement of these gifts and callings within the Body, but it also does not take away from their own personal calling and assignment.

Pastor Wayne has learned "to be much for God, is to be much with God," and this is evident within the pages of this book. We are made aware that God is not just asking, "Who will go for Us?" but also "Who will go with Us?" The equipment to make that journey successfully can be found within the nine chapters of this present age needed book. Read it prayerfully, eagerly, but carefully. Your future ministry light will shine the brighter for it!

Dr. Leslie M. Brown
Higher Ground Ministries

Pastor Wayne Hancock is able to capture a powerful message in his book, *You Are Called to Him and for Him*. This book contains all of the key ingredients that are necessary for anyone to truly understand what it means to be called of God and how that calling is to function in harmony with the Body of Christ, the local church, and the ministry of their Pastor.

We are all called to do great things for God and discovering that calling is vital if we are to be chosen by Him for service. This book will resonate in the heart of every believer who is seeking God's calling and provides practical advice on how to effectively fulfill our purpose.

Anyone who is serious about pursuing God with a passion, I highly recommend this book to you. To pastors, *You Are Called to Him and for Him* will provide an excellent tool to develop your leadership team and staff to be healthy, strong, and committed to God, their pastors, and the God-given vision of your ministry.

This book contains a message that people in the Body of Christ have been needing to hear. Thank you Pastor Wayne for giving us this beautiful master key!

Dr. Joshua Bulger
West Coast Believers Center International
www.wcbci.org

I first met Wayne Hancock in 1991 when he visited my home in Tulsa, Oklahoma with his soon to be wife, Robyn, whom I have known since she was a child. Wayne is a good guy and a good minister of the gospel. He has looked to me as a spiritual father and mentor for all these years.

Read his book *You Are Called to Him and for Him*, and then read it again and let it minister to you. The Word of God tells us to make our calling and election sure. It also tells us to work worthy of the vocation where we are called. Whether we are ministers, a layperson, have a ministry job, or a secular job, we must see it as a calling and then fulfill it.

Dr. Terry L. Mize
Terry Mize Ministries

www.terrymizeministries.org

The modern church is faced with the age-old struggle between the grace of God and the performance-oriented mindset. In this book, Wayne Hancock skillfully and scripturally reveals the pitfall of letting *working* for the Lord take the place of *worshipping* the Lord, while at the same time demonstrating the undeniable truth and benefit of faithfulness. *You Are Called to Him and for Him* is a handbook for all who seek a deep and satisfying walk with God.

Rev. Scott Webb
Webb Ministries
www.webbmin.org

Contents

Chapter 1:   Who Is Called? 17
Chapter 2:   Where Are You?...............25
Chapter 3:   The Relationship and Ministry
             Connection...................35
Chapter 4:   Employed to be Deployed.......45
Chapter 5:   The Call, the Kingdom, and the
             Provision 51
Chapter 6:   The Present Call of God 61
Chapter 7:   Stay at Your Post 71
Chapter 8:   Engraved by God..............83
Chapter 9:   The Character and Love
             Connection...................91

Introduction

I was born into this world on September 26, 1968, as the first child to extremely young parents. It wasn't until November 1, 1987 that I first answered the call to the ministry and got baptized with the mighty Holy Spirit. That is when I realized the depth that the hand of God had been on my life for years. You see, I had come from a broken home where my parents divorced when I was at a very young age. My grandparents and great grandparents eventually took me in and raised me on their farm in the hills of Kentucky.

Nobody in my immediate family seemed remotely interested in God or His church, even though they professed to be Christians. My mother tells me that before my parents divorced, I used to take my two younger brothers, Jon and Jason, to the screened-in back porch and I would play church with them. I would prop my Bible on a stool and make my two younger brothers sit down in front of me and I was their pastor.

I later remember, after my parents' bitter divorce, lying on the grass as a small boy in front of my great grandparents' house. I was sorely upset because my small life seemed to be in shambles, even before it really got started. As I laid there on my back and stared up at the clouds questioning and reasoning in my mind about who loved me and who didn't love me, I remember wondering if God was truly real.

Lying there looking at the blue sky and watching the clouds roll by, it was then that I first remember the Lord making Himself real to me. I really didn't know Him, but He unquestionably knew me. Very quickly, as all of these thoughts and questions came regarding my small existence, other people's love for me, and the reality of God, the presence of God fell on me in an all-consuming way that Kentucky day. God made His presence and love known to me at that moment in a very special way. He was there and had always been there, in spite of all the questions and doubts that flooded this little boy's small but growing mind.

Even though I continued to face very difficult and challenging situations as I grew to adulthood, the grace of God was upon my life. At one time, I was driven to the point of suicide as a teenager. In the middle of my great grandparents' driveway, with the barrel of my .22 caliber rifle placed on my forehead and the trigger ready, I was questioning the love of my father, who I barely saw and felt like I didn't really even know. The presence of God seemed so very far away, but He was most definitely present.

It was the hand of God that saw me through a difficult and very rocky start to my life. I was called, but I didn't understand or know it at the time. Satan did his best to hinder me many times throughout those early years of my life, but the goodness of God saw

Introduction

me through. There was and still is a call to be fulfilled, my call *to Him*, as well as my call *for Him*.

In August of 1991, I moved to Broken Arrow, Oklahoma to sit under the ministry of the late Kenneth E. Hagin and to attend RHEMA Bible College. Within days of arriving at school, I ran into a beautiful brown-eyed girl named Robyn. She, too, was part of the call of God upon my life. Robyn became my best friend, and then we later married on July 31, 1993. The hand of God was upon her life and saw her through many difficulties, even as growing up as a pastor's daughter. Our individual calls soon became one call — we both desired to know the Lord and to make Him known by all.

It's amazing to see how the Lord can bring a farm boy from the hills of Kentucky and cause his path to cross with a young lady who was literally raised on the other side of the world on a small island in the middle of the vast Pacific Ocean. The Lord really does know what He's doing, and He really does know how to lead us, sometimes even unawares to us. Trust Him always. Robyn is my closest confidant and friend in this world of ours. We share this journey unto complete fulfillment of the call of God – *to Him* and *for Him*.

Many of us have had rocky starts to our lives. You might even consider your entire life up until this point to be a rocky one with many ups and downs and difficult things you've had to endure. However, it's important to know that it's not over. Satan may have done his best to hinder you from fulfilling the call of God on your life, but he hasn't yet succeeded because you're still breathing. As long as you are breathing, you have an opportunity to know the God that already knows you. To know Him, is to know His love — a love without conditions.

We've all heard it said many times that life is a journey, and it truly is. Sometimes it doesn't seem like a very pleasant journey, but it is a journey nonetheless. Your call is also a journey. You never end up where you start out. We progress in the call of God. It is my prayer that this book will somehow help you along life's journey toward and into the call of God. I want to encourage you that no matter where you may be in the process, to keep going and moving forward. We've all wanted to quit many times, but quitting should never be an option for any of us. Don't give up, because you can and will make it if you refuse to quit.

In the end, we always win.

Wayne Hancock
Maui, Hawaii, U.S.A.

Therefore I, a prisoner for serving the Lord,
beg you to lead a life worthy of your calling,
for you have been called by God.
Ephesians 4:1 (NLT)

Chapter 1

Who Is Called?

Ephesians 4:1 (NLT) — **1** Therefore I, a prisoner for serving the Lord, beg you to lead a life worthy of your calling, for you have been called by God.

Who is called? The answer is a very simple one. *You* are called of God. Called to do what? That's the first thing most people think of when they begin to ponder the call of God. Each of us is called to do something, but what we are called to do is secondary to Whom we are called. We are called *to* God before we are called to do anything *for* God.

You have been handpicked for an intimate relationship with the Heavenly Father, and out of that relationship will come forth God's bespoke plan that has been divinely crafted specifically for you to fulfill. You have been called of God and it's important that you live your life worthy of that calling. Many have understood the call of God and have pursued this call, while many others have yet to answer the call, and multitudes of others simply will not conduct their lives worthy of their Heavenly call. It's all a matter of *our* choice and not God's.

In my experience and travels, I've seen much confusion and many misunderstandings in the Body of Christ regarding the call of God. Many times we put the emphasis regarding God's call for our lives in the wrong place because we don't understand the proper order. If we put undue emphasis on what we have been called to do *for* God, we run the risk of yielding to ungodly pride. Consequently, our relationship with the Lord, and even others, could possibly end up shipwrecked.

Quite frequently, people put the work of God before the God of the work. Or, we could also say it this way: we sometimes put the call *of* God before the call *to* God because we don't understand that there is a vast difference between the two. The call *to* God speaks of our individual relationship *with* God, while the call *of* God speaks of our relationship in the servitude of God toward others in the earth. We must understand the divine order of this call and walk worthy of it. We are first called *to* God before anything else. If this order is switched, then we can end up confused, and consequently, not truly fulfill the full plan *of* God.

Matthew 22:14 (AMP) 14 For many are called (invited and summoned), but few *are* chosen.

I really like how the Amplified version of the Bible clarifies and amplifies this particular verse of Holy Scripture. It refers to the *called* as those who are *invited and summoned*. When God calls a person, He is actually giving them an invitation. To be invited means that we can choose whether or not we accept the invitation. This word *called* is further clarified when the word *summoned* is used to help us better understand its meaning. When we are *summoned*, we can still choose whether or not we are going to respond to this summons. However, there can be dire consequences both in this life as well as the life to come for not having the proper response to this Heavenly summons. Our response to the call of God matters, both in this life and the life still yet to come.

The Bible is very plain in letting us know that many are called. Remember, we are all called of God, but few are actually chosen. *Who are the ones chosen?* They are the ones who have accepted the divine invitation. They have responded to this summons from Heaven to a rich relationship with the Lord, and then they qualified themselves through growing in their relationship with the Lord to be chosen or sent forth to do something for Him on a grander scale.

There's a phrase that is thrown around a lot and is very often used as an excuse for not walking worthy of our divine call. Many times people have used this phrase to not live right and conduct themselves in an unrighteous manner that is not conducive to the call of God. The phrase goes something like this, *"God doesn't call the qualified."* There is a great truth to this phrase. In regards to myself, I definitely wasn't qualified when I received the call of God. No, He most assuredly doesn't call the qualified, but if we are going to be chosen to be used in a mighty way *for* the Kingdom of God in the earth, then we must understand that there is a qualification process that we must all fulfill. God never calls the qualified, but He does expect the called to eventually become qualified.

Thank God for His amazing grace that assists us daily in this qualification process. In other words, there's a God-ward side to the call of God and then there's a man-ward side to the call of God. *God doesn't call the qualified, but He does expect the called to eventually become qualified.* God always does His part, but we must do ours as well, and His grace is what empowers us to grow spiritually in our ever-growing and expanding relationship with the Lord. God supplies the call and the grace; we must supply the humility along with teachableness in order to walk worthy of this divine call.

Why is it that many people don't become *chosen* or *qualified*? I'm convinced that it's because we don't fully understand the call of God. We don't understand *who* is called, what it *means* to be called, and what it *takes* in order to fulfill that call. It is paramount that we understand this in order to truly embrace and fulfill God's call to us.

When we hear this term *called*, generally the very first thought that goes through people's minds is the call of God upon a person as a pastor or evangelist. These ministry gifts are outlined to us in Ephesians.

Ephesians 4:11-12 (NLT) 11 Now these are the gifts Christ gave to the church: the **apostles**, the **prophets**, the **evangelists**, and the **pastors** and **teachers**. **12** Their responsibility is to equip God's people to do his work and build up the church, the Body of Christ.

It's true that there is a call of God for someone to be an apostle, prophet, evangelist, pastor, or teacher, but that's only part of those whom God calls and considers as gifts. Notice in this verse that the responsibility of these apostles, prophets, evangelists, pastors, and teachers is *to equip (or teach) God's people to work*. In other words, there are people who are called, gifted, trained, and qualified to work *for* God who aren't necessarily apostles, prophets, evangelists, pastors, or teachers. If you aren't careful, you can put too much emphasis on those who stand behind the pulpit as the only ones who are gifts of God's grace in the Body of Christ. There are many, many more who are called of God to function in other capacities.

Personally speaking, I am a gift of God's grace in the Body of Christ, but I'm not this gift because I stand behind the pulpit and minister God's Word. I am this gift because this is the grace that has been given to me from the Lord. This is my call *for* Him. This is my part in the Body of Christ. This is my gift *for* His church. I am not a gift because I'm something special in my own eyes, but it's because of the Lord's amazing grace.

There are those whom the Lord has favored me to pastor throughout the years (both locally and around the world) who are gifts in the church. They are gifts *for* the rest of the Body of Christ just as much as I am a gift. Our gifts, or graces, are different in function, but they are still both necessary. One grace gift (those who stand behind the pulpit) seems to get more attention than the other gifts, but that doesn't make them more important or better than the others because they are <u>all</u> needful. We all have our respective places in the Body of Christ. Not only am I a gift to my church, but you are a gift in the church ministry in which the Lord has assigned or called you to work and be a productive part to your spiritual family together with your pastor.

There are far more people who are called to do God's work than there are who speak from a pulpit to a congregation. There are more people in the pew than in the actual pulpit. Ministering from a public speaking position or a pulpit is only one part or facet regarding the work we do *for* God. We are all called to work *for* the Kingdom of God. This applies to every Christian without exception and without fail.

I have encountered a lot of people in my ministry *for* the Lord who think they are called to a pulpit or public ministry, when they aren't really called at all to a pulpit ministry. Even if they are genuinely called to assist from the pulpit in the form of speaking to people, that still doesn't make them an apostle, prophet, evangelist, pastor, or teacher.

There are more people who are called to help or assist those who stand behind the pulpit than those who are actually called to the pulpit as their main ministry. We must never look at one as being more important than the other because they are all equally important and valuable. If everybody stood behind the pulpit, then we wouldn't have anybody to equip to do the other work of the ministry in reaching this world for Christ.

Personally speaking, I am very leery of those who are continually looking for a church pulpit to minister from. Many times it can be pride that drives people to want this position so that they can receive the recognition and validation of man. More times than not, it's often the one who doesn't really want a public ministry that has been called or graced to minister in this capacity. Why? It's because then it's truly the grace or divine ability of the Holy Spirit at work in and through this person. They aren't dependent upon their own natural abilities, but lean heavily upon the ability or grace of God. I am comfortable in my grace, but I am not comfortable in my own ability. In my own self, I am not comfortable ever standing behind a pulpit or ministering to countless people through the written page. It is most definitely the grace of the Lord and we should never lose sight of that.

I have found that there are many people who want to have a ministry title such as *pastor* in order to be seen as valuable in the Body of Christ or society. Here's something vitally important that we must understand and never forget regarding those whom the Lord has called: a calling doesn't mean that you have to have a title in front of your name. Much of the time, this title only feeds ungodly pride in a person's heart because he wants to feel superior to others who don't have a title.

Why does this happen? It can happen because of pride or lust for a particular ministry position that makes one feel important. However, this can also happen because we don't fully understand that we are *all* called of God and are gifts in particular. Each of our positions in the Kingdom of God may be a little different, but they are all valuable and important in fulfilling the plan of God in the earth, no matter what our title, position, or grace might be.

The pulpit ministry is only one part of the whole regarding the call of God. The call of God is for everybody. So it's vital that we understand *who* is called, and that's everybody. It's also important to know what it means to be called, what we are called to do, and what it takes in order to actually fulfill that call.

Many people live and die and never fully understand God's call. Therefore, they don't totally fulfill all that He's called them to in the earth. I don't want that to ever be said of me, as well as for those whom the Lord has entrusted under my spiritual guidance and leadership as a ministerial gift in the Body of Christ.

The purpose of this book is to better equip you in understanding the call of God and to help you along the way in fulfilling whatever it is that He has invited, summoned, or *called* you to. I am not writing this book to be an exhaustive study on the various ministry gifts as there are many of those already available. My prayer is that this book will help point you in the right direction concerning God's call for your life. Each of our individual calls will be different, even though they are all spiritually intertwined and connected.

Chapter 2

Where Are You?

If you have spent any time at all studying the Bible, you are familiar with the creation and fall of man. I love to study the book of Genesis because I believe this book helps give us a very clear understanding of God's original intent or will for His man. It reveals God's original plan—for man to have a relationship with Him and to live and walk in the BLESSING on a daily basis.

In Genesis chapter one we find the history of the creation of the earth and then we see the creation of man, which is the Father's most important and highest creation. In Genesis chapter two we find out about man's life and responsibility in the Garden of Eden. Then in Genesis chapter three we see the temptation and eventual fall of man.

Most everybody knows the account of when Adam and Eve sinned and what transpired after that. However, there's something in the middle of this that we very often overlook that applies to us today. Do you remember the very first thing that the Lord said when He came looking for fellowship or some personal one-on-one time with His man?

Genesis 3:8-9 (NLT) 8 When the cool evening breezes were blowing, the man and his wife heard the LORD God walking about in the garden. So they hid from the LORD God among the trees. **9** Then the LORD God called to the man, "Where are you?"

We understand that the Lord is omniscient, which simply means that He is all-knowing. He knows everything about us, more than we even know or realize about ourselves. He's God and that makes Him all-knowing. In His omniscience, He knew exactly the physical whereabouts of His man. He knew exactly what bush Adam and Eve were hiding behind.

We also know that Adam and Eve had a responsibility to tend and guard the Garden of Eden. We know that they had charge over the Garden and everything in it. It's interesting to note that the first words out of the Lord's mouth were not *"What in the world have you done? Why did you eat of My tree? Why didn't you cast the devil out of this Garden and protect it from the likes of the evil one? Why aren't you doing what I called you to do in the earth?"*

God's first response to man's sin was very simply, *"Where are you?"* I believe that this is the very same response that our Father has toward many people still today, *"Where are you?"*

It's important that we examine our hearts and begin to think soberly where we are today. In other words, where are we in regards to our relationship with the Lord our Creator? Where are we in our walk with Him? Where are we with our call?

The Lord came walking in the Garden of Eden with one thing on His heart and mind. He was eager to see and walk with man. He was excited to embrace His man and simply spend some personal time loving and laughing together with them, but Adam and Eve weren't there. When the Lord said, "Where are you?" one aspect of what He was speaking was in terms of Adam's relationship with Him. He was calling His man. The Lord came to the Garden of Eden with one thing in mind and that was to *walk* with His man, but He ended up taking a walk all by Himself instead.

Where are you today? Where are you with your walk with the Lord? Where are you in regards to your relationship with the One Who loves you most? He loves you more than the ministry, more than the people of your church, more than the people who live in your household, and more than the people at your workplace. Where is your walk with the Lord today? Where are you in your call *to* Him?

Genesis 3:9 (NLT) 9 Then the LORD God called to the man, "Where are you?"

All the Lord has ever truly wanted from Adam was love and fellowship. This was, and still is, God's *call* to man: to simply be *with* Him. Then everything else would be fulfilled in the process (such as the exercising of authority and dominion in the Garden of Eden, and replenishing the entire planet).

There is a valid call *to do* certain things for the Lord, such as standing in a particular five-fold ministry office as an apostle, prophet, evangelist, pastor, or teacher, as well as those who have been called to function within the ministry of helps (which I believe is probably the most important). The ministry of helps simply means that you have been called to help those who stand in these various ministry offices or gifts. It means that you've been called to assist these ministry gifts in fulfilling their calls in the earth of equipping the Body of Christ for the work of the ministry.

On the flip side of this, the five-fold ministry offices of the apostle, prophet, evangelist, pastor, and teacher are called to help you fulfill what you've been called to do for the Lord. We are all called to assist each other in our work *for* the Lord. However, as important as all of this is, it's still not as important as man's primary call, and that primary call is the call *to* Him. It's a call of relationship.

Many times we allow things to come between us and our primary or first call and that is *to* Him. Before you are ever called *to do*, you are first called *to be* – to be with Him. It's in your being with Him, that you'll receive the equipping and revelation that you'll need in order to fulfill what you've been called to do *for* Him with much greater grace and ease.

Where are you? Are you out of your position? Are you in hiding behind a bush? How's your relationship with the Lord? Don't allow anything to come between you and your first and primary call to be with Him.

Mark 3:13-19 (AMP) 13 And He went up on the hillside and called to Him [for Himself] those whom He wanted *and* chose, and they came to Him. **14** And He appointed twelve to continue to be with Him, and that He might send them out to preach [as apostles or special messengers] **15** And to have authority *and* power to *heal the sick and to* drive out demons: **16** [They were] Simon, and He surnamed [him] Peter; **17** James son of Zebedee and John the brother of James, and He surnamed them Boanerges, that is, Sons of Thunder; **18** And Andrew, and Philip, and Bartholomew (Nathaniel), and Matthew, and Thomas, and James son of Alphaeus, and Thaddaeus (Judas, not Iscariot), and Simon the Cananaean [also called Zelotes], **19** And Judas Iscariot, he who betrayed Him.

I absolutely love how the Amplified version of this scripture clarifies what Jesus did and is saying in these holy verses. Notice it says that He called those to Him *for Himself*.

The calling of God for your life is connected with Him, and unless you are connected with Him, you will have a hard time knowing and fulfilling whatever it is that the Master has called you to do *for* Him. He has called you *for Himself*. You were created *for* Him.

I also love the way that those whom Jesus called were appointed *to continue to be with Him*. You aren't called to just visit Him every once in a great while, but you are called to be with Him continually.

Jesus wants you to be in His presence. He wants your fellowship. He desires to love and to be loved by you, and to love the world through you. The only way that the Lord will be able to love the world through you (for you to be a witness and preach the gospel), is by you continuing to be with Him.

It will be far easier for you to love the people of this world with God's unconditional love, when you are continually in the presence of the One Who loves you the most. If you ever find yourself having difficulty loving others in this world, you need to do a checkup on your own relationship with the Lord. Those who spend time with the Master and experience His unconditional love toward them will likewise love the people of this world with that same kind of love.

It will be easy to demonstrate the healing power of God to a world in need of healing, when you are continually in the presence of the Healer Himself. To know Him is to know the Healer and the great Healer will show you how to flow in the power of the Spirit.

It's easy to demonstrate the power of God to truly prosper financially, when you are continually in the presence of the Provider Himself. He will show you how. To know Him is to know His financial provision. Those who don't know His provision really don't know Him because you cannot separate God from His provision. To know Him is to know His power!

Our relationship with the Lord should be strong and true. Our time spent in the Father's presence should be our number one priority. This is one way we seek first the Kingdom or call of God, by spending time with the God of the call. When you know the God and Father of the call, you will know greater details of what He has called you to do in the world in the lives of others. The details and fulfillment of the call of God will come easy for those who spend time with and know the Caller. He has called you to be *with* Him, and by being *with* Him, His call for your life to affect the world around you will be revealed in grand and glorious detail, along with the steps that you need to take in order to fulfill that call in the earth.

Did you ever wonder why Jesus handpicked these particular twelve men to be with Him? Was it because of their social or economic status? Was it because of their educational background or college degree? Was it because they were eloquent speakers?

The answer to all of these questions is an obvious *No*. Why did He pick these twelve men? It was simply because these twelve men had first responded to a previous call to simply follow Him. It was in their following Him that they had developed a greater hunger for Him and His presence. They longed to be with the Master, and the Master longed to be with them. Therefore, these twelve had a place with Him that others didn't have.

We progress in the call of God, whatever that call may be for our lives. You don't generally end up where you begin. We should continually be making progress in our walk with the Master. It's in our being with Him that we are able to receive further instructions and revelation as to what the Lord has called us to do *for* Him, which is secondary to simply being *with* Him.

When these twelve began to consecrate themselves to the call and will of God, the Lord was able to give them specific and detailed instructions as to what He called them to do for Him. First, we are called *to* Him. This is our primary call, to be *with* Him.

Second, we are called to service, or to be sent out from His holy presence and take what was received and learned there and help others. These twelve were sent out to preach, exercise authority, and given power to heal the sick and drive out demons only after they had been with Him. One should never try to preach, or to do anything *for* the Lord, unless he has first spent time *with* Him by developing a strong relationship.

Jesus spent the first thirty years of His life by answering and putting His primary call to be with His Father first and foremost. He spent the first thirty years of His life's calling cultivating His relationship with the Father. Before the Father sent Him out from His presence to do something *for* Him, He was first *with* Him. It's also interesting to note that it took Him only about three years to accomplish what the Lord called Him to do *for* Him. It was in those first thirty years that He found out Who He really was and received the revelation in specific details as to what He was to do *for* the Father in regards to the redemption of mankind. The first thirty years of His life and ministry were first *to* the Father before He ever ministered *for* Him publicly. Before He ever ministered publicly, He first ministered to and received ministry from His Father.

It took Jesus thirty years of preparation for three years of ministry. Why is man so eager sometimes to jump out there before he's ready to jump? We must take time to be with Him before we ever try to produce any lasting fruit for the Kingdom of God. Before one is ever called to do anything *for* the Lord, he is first called *to be with* the Lord. It's not so much about doing as it is in being.

Think about this for a moment. What exactly is Christianity all about? Is it about winning the world to Jesus and getting the entire planet born-again? Is Christianity all about getting sick bodies healed by the power of God? Is Christianity all about putting money in one's pocket? No, the primary basis for Christianity is simply being with Him (the Lord), and as we are with Him, He then sends us forth to help introduce others to this One Whom we know and love so dearly. It's hard to preach the gospel of the Lord Jesus Christ to introduce others to salvation if you barely know the Lord yourself.

This is why many people don't have a true or lasting passion for the things of God or public ministry because it stems out of the depth of one's relationship with Him. I've seen many people start out in their walk with the Lord and had intentions on doing great things for Him, who initially had lots of passion, but eventually end up passionless. Why? It's because the depth of their relationship with the Lord is short-lived. It's too shallow.

Chapter 3

The Relationship and Ministry Connection

If you ever find yourself losing passion for what the Lord has called you to do for Him, it's possibly because you've lost your passion to be with Him. It's in your being with Him that you will have a strong passion to accomplish whatever it is that He has called you to do for Him... even with our continual dealings and experiencing many kinds of hurts from other Christians along the way. It's a strong relationship with the Lord that enables you to keep on going, loving, and reaching out to people even when some of these people cause hurt and pain.

As a pastor, I can clearly see symptoms of people's lack of relationship with the Lord through their attitude toward others and the ministry. It will also show up in their attitude in fulfilling their responsibilities or tasks they are given to accomplish at church.

When you begin to renege on what you know you are supposed to be doing for the church, it could be simply because you aren't strong in your relationship or walk with Him. When you are strong in your relationship with God, then you'll not forget the things or responsibilities that you have volunteered to oversee and been assigned to do by your pastor. When you are strong in your relationship with the Lord, it can help you follow through with your commitments of service in the work of the Lord. When your relationship with the Lord is strong, then you aren't looking for excuses to get out of doing something for your church. When your relationship with the Lord is strong, you'll not look for excuses for not giving the church your very best all of the time.

Time and time again, I have seen people commit and give their word to do a certain thing, but then not follow through with their commitment because they've allowed other things to capture their attention. Why? In my experience, it's simply because it's not important enough to them. Many times the commitments we make are half-hearted, and we may end up not fulfilling those commitments because we aren't first fully committed to Him.

I realize that these are strong statements, but when we are committed to Him, our words of commitment to others (including our pastor and the church) will always be fulfilled and fulfilled in the time that we said we would do them. Many times people don't follow through with their commitments at church because they don't follow through on their commitment first to be with Him, the Lord of the church. The depth of your relationship with the Lord will often be reflected in the depth of your passion to be involved in your local church by helping your pastor.

Usually, it's the truth that offends or hurts people's feelings. I'm not trying to hurt anybody's feelings, but I earnestly desire the Holy Spirit to begin to reveal things in your heart that really need to be revealed and will be a blessing to you.

When your relationship or walk with the Lord is your number one priority, then your service for the Lord will come easy. Our service to the Lord and His church come easy when our hearts are flooded with His divine presence. Our hearts can only be flooded by His divine presence by spending time in His presence. Yes, we must read the Word of God, but in addition to our reading and studying the Word of God, we must take time to simply sit in His holy presence through prayer. We must have a greater hunger for the presence of the Lord in our lives. It's imperative that we continually cultivate a strong relationship with the Lord.

Let your words be weighty when you speak them. Mean what you say and then follow through with your responsibilities and commitments to the work of the Lord. If you tell your pastor that you're going to do something for him, then follow through without being asked about it a second or third time. Otherwise, your pastor will have to start looking elsewhere for his needed assistance. If you tell somebody at church, in your particular department of ministry, that you are going to do something, then make sure you do it and do it as unto the Lord.

I'm endeavoring to show you the connection between our relationship *with* the Lord, and what we are called to do *for* Him. It will be difficult for you to *do* things for the Lord (long-term), if your commitment *to* the Lord in your personal relationship with Him isn't strong. Our roots must go down deep and strong in Him. It's important that we answer the call to be with Him, so that we can accomplish those things that we have been called to accomplish in the earth. When your relationship with the Lord is number one, then your duties and obligations (to the Work of the Lord) won't take a back seat to other things.

I do realize that sometimes we may make commitments that we can't keep, even though our intentions were right in the beginning. It's in these times that we must learn how to ask for help, or simply let the one that we have committed ourselves to, know that we won't be able to fulfill what we had previously committed ourselves to do. Yes, we do live in a very busy world. Sometimes our work schedules change, as well as family needs. However, you must still be honorable enough to let your church leaders know where you are and what's going on, so that the work of the Lord doesn't suffer lack in the process. Be mindful to never be considered by your pastor or church leaders as AWOL (absent without leave).

Mark 3:13-15 (MSG) 13 He climbed a mountain and invited those he wanted with him. They climbed together. **14** He settled on twelve, and designated them apostles. The plan was that they would be with him, and he would send them out to proclaim the Word **15** and give them authority to banish demons.

The Relationship and Ministry Connection

When we respond to the invitation of Jesus to be with Him and are passionate in this relationship, we will be passionate about doing things for Him. When we respond to the Master's invitation to be with Him, then He can speak to us in minute detail the things which He wants us to do for Him. When we answer the call to be with Him, then we can be chosen to accomplish great things for Him in the earth. This is the divine order that God has established in His Word. First, we are called to be *with* Him. Second, in our being *with* Him, we can be sent out from His presence full of His wisdom, grace, and power to accomplish those things which He has called us to accomplish *for* Him.

Many are called or invited, but few actually show up and are accounted for. Make sure you are one of those who show up, and then you can be chosen to do great things for God based out of your relationship with Him, not out of duty or obligation.

You have been called *to* Him. Don't ever lose sight of this all important truth. Continually ask yourself, "Where am I in my relationship with the Lord?" Always be truthful and honest with yourself. Don't deceive yourself into thinking that your relationship is strong, when it isn't. Don't allow other things to come between you and your walk with the Lord, such as an unsubmitted heart, which will manifest through the lust for other things.

What is lust? Lust is simply a strong desire to have something that is outside of the will of God for your life. Sometimes our lust can be for physical things, feelings, emotions, or even people. Sometimes we can have an ungodly attitude and even look for hurts and offenses from other people, including our church leaders.

Many times it almost appears that some people seem to go through life expecting others to offend them. They are just waiting to get their feelings hurt. If you look for these things and begin to expect them to happen to you, then you will have plenty of them. In your finding them, you can and will lose sight of your call to be with Him and your place in the work of the Kingdom of God in the earth. I've seen many Christians through all my years of pastoring who eventually end up with an AWOL status, and it all started with an offense or hurt.

When you are continually with Him, there won't be room for hurt, offense, or bitterness. There will only be room for love, regardless of how others may treat you. There will only be room for mercy and forgiveness.

Through the years, I've seen people get hurt and offended at others in the church world, and then see their relationship with the Lord suffer because they chose to allow something to get under their skin. I've had many great men of God tell me that one must be thick-skinned, but at the same time tenderhearted.

The truth is, as long as we are in this world, opportunities for offenses and hurts will come our way. It's how we respond during these times that is critical. When your relationship with the Lord is strong, then it makes no difference if it seems as if the entire world has turned against you. Your relationship with the Lord won't suffer, and you'll continue to keep the commitments that you've made in helping further establish the Kingdom of God in the earth, even cleaning the toilets at church.

The devil is always looking for people that he can take out. His primary objective is to separate or divert you from the plan of God. The enemy also wants to bring division in your relationship with your pastor and the church. You have the responsibility to guard and protect the plan of God for your life. Don't take the devil's bait of offense and allow yourself to be hurt or offended.

I heard a great man of God say once, "It's okay if you have a 'moment,' but just make sure that it's just exactly that, a 'moment.'" There will be an initial effect or shock of somebody's actions or what they have said, but don't let that disappointment stick to you and sink down into your heart. It will cause a root of bitterness to spring up toward that other person, and especially toward the Lord and His work. Be thick-skinned and tenderhearted. Remember, you are called to be with Him, and in your being with Him, He will show you how to handle any disappointment, offense, or hurt that others may bring your way.

Always make it a priority to continually pray for those whom the Lord has placed over your life as a spiritual covering, primarily your pastor. As a pastor, it is very easy for me to tell who prays and who doesn't pray. It's even easier for me to tell who actually prays for me and who doesn't pray for me. Prayer will always produce a spiritual intimacy with the one for whom you are praying.

When you are continually praying for your pastors and leaders, you are loving them in the spirit. You will develop a deep love and spiritual intimacy for the one you pray for. You are investing love in them. No matter what this person says or does that could possibly cause hurt or offense in your life, you will not become hurt or offended. If you do, it will be for only a short season of time. Why? It's because you love that person deeply with the pure love of God, and the love of God will always forgive when it suffers a wrong.

Sometimes the hurts and offenses that we suffer are simply because we perceived something wrongly. Insecurity will always breed hurt and offense. Let me say this in context with what we are talking about. Insecurity in your relationship with the Lord will open up the door for you to experience hurt and offense from God's people. When you fail to pray as you should, you can find yourself on track to experience hurt and offense.

Your number one priority or calling is to fulfill the plan of God for your life at all costs. Your number one calling isn't your job. Your number one calling isn't your position at church. Your number one calling isn't to minister to the multitudes. All of these are important and are part of the plan of God, but they're not the foundation for which your life or ministry is to be built upon.

The foundation for your life, plan, and calling of God is to be with Him, and in your being with Him, to actually know Him. It's as you know Him that you can then begin to find out what else you have been called to do and fulfill. However, your main quest in life in

The Relationship and Ministry Connection

fulfilling the Father's plan is to know the Father of the plan. You are called to be with Him.

Here's the Father's call for your life and where you are to start in discovering what the Father has called you to do from Mark 3:13-15 from the Bible. This is listed in order of importance because every call of God can only be fulfilled when it's based upon the sure foundation of knowing Him, in consequence of continually being with Him.

1. To be with Him (through the reading of the Bible, prayer, and even fasting)
2. To preach the gospel (or witness)
3. To know and demonstrate the power of God

The plan of God for your life is that you first be with Him. This is where you start and your number one priority. Everything else is secondary regardless of whatever else it is that you are called to do in the future. When you are with Him, by spending time with Him in His written Word, and in prayer, you will have a greater foundation to be a witness and preach the gospel to those who don't know Him, whether this is behind the pulpit or simply being a Christian and sharing the Good News with others at your workplace, business, or personal affairs.

When you are with Him, you will begin to understand more and more about His glorious power and how to release His power to a world in need. Miracles, signs, and wonders follow those who believe, not just those who are called to stand behind a pulpit. Miracles will follow those who have spent time in the holy presence of the Lord. It's easy to believe Him when you spend time in His life-changing presence.

Your passion for the things of God and His work will grow out of your passionate relationship with the Lord. There is a direct connection between your passion in your relationship with the Lord and your work for the Lord. If you don't have a passionate relationship with the Lord, then you're not going to be very passionate about what you do for Him and His Kingdom on the earth. Guard your passion for Him at all costs. Be passionate *toward* the Lord, and then you'll be passionate *for* the Lord.

Chapter 4

Employed to be Deployed

The call of God is the plan of God. To know your call is to know His plan. If we are passionate about the call of God, then we are passionate about knowing and fulfilling the Father's plan. There isn't one person, calling, or gifting that is better than any of the others in the Body of Christ. This goes for both the pulpit and the pew. There isn't one person who is insignificant in the plan of God and each and every one has a holy responsibility to fulfill that plan. Everybody has a place.

We've all been called to fulfill His plan, which begins first by simply being with Him on a daily basis. Second, we've all been called to accomplish something for Him in the earth. We are all called to Him, and we are all called to do something for Him.

Whether you are called as an apostle, prophet, evangelist, pastor, or teacher, or simply called to assist these ministry offices or gifts, you are called to do something very important for Him.

It's easy to look at the lives of others who may be in the spotlight of the pulpit, and then view ourselves as unimportant and not really called to do anything for the Lord. This simply isn't true. Everybody is called in one way or another. You may never grace the pulpit in a church setting or a gospel crusade to hundreds of thousands of people, but you may be called to grace the helm of running a business to help finance the gospel. You may be called and graced to raise a house full of Godly children. Remember, you aren't just raising a child, you are raising a call.

If you aren't called to work in the ministry full-time with the ministry being your main source of income, you may be called to be a school custodian, auto body repair man, or even a landscaper. Maybe you are called to teach children in our school system, or maybe you're called to be a financial investor. It makes no difference. Whatever it is that the Lord has called you to do, the main reason why the Lord has you doing that particular assignment is to help people and to be a light in a dark world. In this light, you are actually called to full-time ministry, even though you may work as a kindergarten teacher. You are there to reach people with the love of God. You aren't just there to get a paycheck. Be mindful of this daily.

Maybe the Lord will assign you to work at a fast food restaurant, but that assignment is for the purpose of reaching others there in that workplace environment. Wherever and whatever it is that you may do in this world, it is ultimately for a higher purpose and that is to reach others with the gospel by loving them into the Kingdom. Your true employment is in Heaven, but your deployment is here on the earth. We must never get these two confused.

The Lord even calls people to be business entrepreneurs to help make money to finance a church by being a blessing to their pastor and his ministry. Everything that we do in this life should be connected to a higher purpose. It should be connected with the call of God.

Personally speaking, I am employed by Heaven and deployed as a pastor in my church and a minister to other peoples and nations. You may be deployed as a baker, but your employment is actually divine and for a Heavenly purpose or call. The financial benefits that you enjoy from your earthly position are secondary to your Kingdom purpose.

The Lord has graced each of us for a specific purpose or plan in the earth. You are part of the Father's plan. Your life matters and is extremely important and critical in the Father's eyes. You were born with a plan attached to your life that can never be separated from you. It's now your responsibility to discover that plan and then to fulfill it to the best of your ability.

We are all called of God and each called into His service in one capacity or another. Callings, or plans, are not put on reserve for only those who are called to a pulpit type of ministry. Actually, pulpit ministry is only a part of the whole of God's plans. In that sense, every Christian is a minister in one capacity or another.

A minister is simply one who serves the needs of others, and as you very well know, the world is full of needs. Everywhere we look we can see all kinds of needs. As the called of God, we are all called to serve God in this world by helping meet the needs of others.

The primary need that we are all called to meet for humanity is to introduce humanity to the love of Jesus Christ and to help develop their relationship (or call to be) with Him. When we keep our priorities straight by first being with the Lord, and second, obeying Him in what He has called us to do in regards to others, all needs can and will eventually become a thing of the past. The Lord is always faithful to meet our material needs when we are putting spiritual things first.

When we increase in our relationship with God, then our physical needs become a thing of the past. Man's greatest need is not financial. Man's greatest need is not healing of a devilish disease. These are both valid needs, but not the greatest need. Many times we are only looking for a quick or temporary fix to our problems, instead of a long-term solution.

Man's greatest need is to renew his mind to know the very thoughts of God concerning the call of the Father. We can only know the thoughts of God by spending time with Him and learning His thoughts. When we spend time with God through His Word, in prayer, and in worship, then our relationship with Him will grow by leaps and bounds. This is God's primary call for every human being—to know Him. It's in knowing Him that we are able to renew our minds (according to Romans 12:1-2) and thereby answer the call to God.

When you were born, no matter the circumstances in which that may have happened, whether positive or negative, there was a plan born with you at the same time. The plan of God was attached to your life the moment you were conceived in your mother's womb.

Your days had been planned and destined before you ever lived a single one of them.

Psalm 139:13-16 (MSG) 13 Oh yes, you shaped me first inside, then out; you formed me in my mother's womb. **14** I thank you, High God—you're breathtaking! Body and soul, I am marvelously made! I worship in adoration—what a creation! **15** You know me inside and out, you know every bone in my body; you know exactly how I was made, bit by bit, how I was sculpted from nothing into something. **16** Like an open book, you watched me grow from conception to birth; all the stages of my life were spread out before you, the days of my life all prepared before I'd even lived one day.

The Lord does have a call or plan *for* you that has existed before you ever took your very first breath in this world. You must know this and settle it in your heart and mind right now. As insignificant or unimportant you may think you are in the grand scheme of things regarding the Kingdom of God, this couldn't be any further from the truth. You are very significant. You are very important.

Your significance and importance are not based upon being from a specific geographical location, having a certain social status, or even of a particular race of people. It's not based upon your nationality or skin color. It's not based upon your education or lack thereof. It's not based upon having a certain economical or financial class or standing. Remember, you are employed by Heaven and have been deployed here in the earth.

Maybe you were deployed as a black man hunting on the African plains; maybe you were deployed as a white man trading stocks in New York City; or maybe you were deployed as a brown man in a remote village in a distant south pacific island. Regardless of your skin color or where you live, your so-called "social status" according to the world's standards means nothing in the Kingdom of God. No matter where or how you were born, you were born with a purpose. When you begin to see this purpose, you'll begin to answer the call of God and fulfill what He has destined for you from the beginning of the ages.

Your significance and importance in the plan or call of God are based entirely upon who the Lord says that you are and your relationship with Him, not what others may say that you are. Once again, I want to tell you that you are very significant and that you are very important to the Lord and to the Body of Christ. You are very important to the fulfillment of the plan of God in the earth, whether you live in a huge city or a tiny village in a very remote part of the world that some may not even be able to locate on a map. The Father knows where you are and He has a big plan for you.

You are significant and important to the Body of Christ. Your call is significant and important in the plan of God. The call of God for your life is the assignment the Lord has given you to fulfill on the earth. It's important that we discover, learn, and fulfill the assignment of God on our lives, and this comes by understanding that we are first called to God. The call of God is the plan of God. We have all been called… called to fulfill our Father's plan.

Chapter 5

The Call, the Kingdom, and the Provision

The Father has big plans for each of us. None of His plans are insignificant or without importance, no matter how we may view whatever it is that He has assigned us to do in the Body of Christ. We must fulfill our Father's plans and not let those plans be hindered or delayed from coming to pass because of our thoughts or feelings, or even the thoughts and feelings of others who may not understand our assignments.

The very first scripture that comes to heart and mind regarding the plan of God is very familiar, but at the same time a very important verse of scripture that we must examine in the light of the subject that we are talking about in this book.

Jeremiah 29:11 (NLT) 11 For I know the plans I have for you," says the LORD. "They are plans for good and not for disaster, to give you a future and a hope."

The very first thing that sticks out to us in this verse is that the Father knows the plans that He has for us. Of course, it's important that He knows these plans, but it's equally important that we find out and know these plans as well. We must discover these important plans in order for us to fulfill those plans.

This verse also tells us that these plans are for good and not for disaster. The Father has good plans for you. Every plan of God is a good plan. He has no bad plans. They are plans for your success and not failure. Let's look at this verse in a couple more translations to help us better understand what the Father is trying to get across to us in this verse.

Jeremiah 29:11 (NET1) 11 For I know what I have planned for you,' says the LORD. 'I have plans to prosper you, not to harm you. I have plans to give you a future filled with hope.

It's wonderful to know that our Father has plans to prosper you and not to harm you. It has never been the Father's plan to harm His children. In other words, we serve a loving Father Who is always looking out for our best interest. He has big plans to give us a bright future that is filled with tremendous hope.

Jeremiah 29:11 (MSG) 11 I know what I'm doing. I have it all planned out—plans to take care of you, not abandon you, plans to give you the future you hope for.

It's so good to know that our Father knows exactly what He's doing in our lives. Not everything that happens to us, especially the bad things that may come our way, come to us *from* the Heavenly Father. It's never been part of the Father's plan for any of His children to die a tragic death from either an accident or from a devilish sickness or disease. This is not the characteristic of a loving Heavenly Father. However, we do know that the devil does his absolute best to try to hinder the plan of God from coming to pass in the earth. The Father's plan is health and healing. The Father's plan is a plan of prosperity not of lack.

The call of God is the call of the Kingdom. It is a call to put the Kingdom of God first in your life, no matter what it is that you have been assigned to do by the Father. God must always come first before anything else. This is part of the divine order of the Father's plan for us.

Our number one priority should never be our secular employment in this world, even though our employment is definitely important to help sustain our financial obligations. Our number one priority in life should be, *"Am I fulfilling my responsibility in the Father's call or plan for my life?"* We must fulfill the plan of Heaven upon the earth. The plan of God must come to pass in the earth and each of us has a part to fulfill in this glorious endeavor.

Matthew 6:33 (NKJV) 33 But seek first the kingdom of God and His righteousness, and all these things shall be added to you.

This is truly one of the most important scriptures in the entire Bible. This verse sums everything up for us. We are to be seeking the Kingdom of God first and foremost before we are to seek any other kingdom. Actually, the Kingdom of God is the only kingdom that truly matters. The Kingdom of God has a plan and that plan must be fulfilled. The Kingdom of God is the plan of God. We must be seeking first the plan of God for our lives above and beyond any other plan. This is the only plan that really matters.

Matthew 6:33 (AMP) 33 But seek (aim at and strive after) first of all His Kingdom and His righteousness (His way of doing and being right), and then all these things taken together will be given you besides.

In other words, we must discover and learn for ourselves God's way of doing things. God's way of doing things is His plan. We must learn to make God's way our way. We must make God's plans our plans. We must live our lives in such a way that the plan of God is always first and foremost in all that we do. This is truly the only cause that really counts, the fulfillment of God's plan.

Proverbs 19:21 (AMP) 21 Many plans are in a man's mind, but it is the Lord's purpose for him that will stand.

There may be many plans in your mind at this moment, but it's only the plan of God that really matters and will truly stand in the very end. The Father is the Master Planner and holds the master plans for your calling. However, it's important to realize that there are actually four different plans that have been laid out for your life, three of which really don't matter. We must pursue the one that matters.

First, there is God's plan. Second, we have the devil's plan. Third, there's your plan. Lastly, even other people have plans for you. Only one of these plans is the correct plan. The last three of these plans really don't matter in the grand scheme of things. It's only the plan of God that has lasting purpose and will truly stand. Nothing else matters but the plan of God. Find out what God's plan is for your life, embrace it, and fulfill it, no matter the cost. The benefits of fulfilling the plan of God extend far beyond this world. Never forget that the Father's plan is the only plan that really matters.

For every Godly plan, there is a supply to fulfill that plan. When we are pursuing the plan of God for our lives instead of our own, every need of ours is taken care of in the process of fulfilling that plan. This could be the reason why so many people struggle to get their physical or financial needs met. If you are pursuing the plan of God, the Father is obligated to supply the needs of that plan. If you aren't pursuing the Father's plan for your life, He isn't obligated to finance that plan.

As long as we are seeking first the Kingdom of God, which is the plan of God, all our needs will be met. Sure, we may experience obstacles along the way. The devil will see to this and will always work overtime to discourage you from fulfilling the Father's plan. He will do his best to try to hinder Heavenly plans from coming to pass. However, if you know your spiritual authority and you know how to truly exercise and use your faith, there isn't a single need that will ever go unmet.

Matthew 6:33 (NLT) 33 Seek the Kingdom of God above all else, and live righteously, and he will give you everything you need.

If you are seeking the Kingdom of God (the plan of God) first and living right, the Father will give you everything that you may ever need. It's the Father's responsibility to finance His plan. He's not obligated to finance a plan that didn't originate with Him, even though that plan may be connected with the ministry. If it's not God's plan, then He's not obligated to fund it.

I have one of the greatest jobs in the whole world. Actually, it's not really a job because it's a calling. It's His plan for my life and ministry here on the earth. He has given me the honor and privilege of being able to meet and minister to many of His precious people around the world: people who are also called, people who also have the plan of God attached to their lives.

Over the course of meeting all of God's wonderful people, it can sometimes get overwhelming because I see so many financial needs that must be met. However, it is so freeing and liberating to know that I am not the one responsible for meeting all of these needs. These precious people that I have met and will continue to meet aren't called to fulfill my plans, and I'm not called to fulfill their plans. However, we are all called to find and fulfill the Father's plans. This means that I'm not obligated financially to meet all of these needs, neither are you. The Heavenly Father is the One Who is obligated, as long as these people are truly walking in His plan and exercising their spiritual authority and faith for the financial provision for the plan.

It's important that the people of God remember where their source of supply is located. The Heavenly Father is your source and your supply. He is The Source that will supply whatever it is that you need in order to fulfill His plans in the earth.

The Call, the Kingdom, and the Provision

Always look to God as your source for your supply and never look to man. It matters not where you live and what limited resources you may think are available to you at the moment. God is not limited because of where you live. God is not limited by your limited resources. God is not limited because of your race. God is not limited in the slightest degree. However, we limit God when we begin to look at our limited resources. We limit our source (the Father) and hinder the supply (the need from being met), when we begin to look toward man instead of God.

Sometimes the Lord has spoken to us to meet certain financial needs that we've seen in other ministries and in various places. As the Lord has directed us (not as man has directed), we've been blessed to be a channel in which the Lord has used us to help build church buildings, purchased church properties, etc. This is truly a very humbling and rewarding experience. However, in each of these occasions, the Lord has specifically spoken to our hearts to help with these needs. We didn't help because people asked us to help.

So many of God's people limit God by putting their focus on another ministry or person to help them fund the call of God on their life as well as the plan attached to it. There's no faith in such thinking. Faith doesn't belong in man; it belongs in God and His Word. He's the Source of all your supply to fulfill the plan of God, not man. Man is only a channel. Be careful to not put undue pressure on people to meet your financial needs because you will then begin to limit God from meeting those needs. Look to your source (God) and don't focus your attention on what man may or may not do for you. Channels may change, but The Source (your Heavenly Father) never changes.

It's perfectly fine to ask others to stand in faith and agreement with you concerning your needs, but be careful that you aren't asking others to pray for you with a wrong motive. Don't ever try to disguise yourself asking for a financial need to be met through an individual by asking them for prayer. If you are genuinely asking them to join their faith with you and to pray with you, that's great. Always make sure your motives are correct when you share your prayer needs with other people.

When you are seeking first the Kingdom of God (the plan of God), all of your needs will be taken care of in the process. Make sure the focus of your heart is in the right place and everything else will be added unto you.

Matthew 6:31 (Phillips NT) 33 Set your heart on the kingdom and his goodness, and all these things will come to you as a matter of course.

When you are on course to fulfill the plan of God, everything that you need in order to fulfill those plans will come to you as a matter of course. We could also say it this way, your needs will be met because you're on course fulfilling the Father's plan. Stay in faith. Exercise your spiritual authority by commanding the devil to take his hands off the money you need, release the angels of God to go get your supply and bring it to you so that you can fulfill the Father's plan. Then from that point forward simply praise God that He has already met those needs.

As long as you continue to confess need instead of provision, needs will continue to be just exactly that, needs. Needs are only met when you learn how to sow the seed of the Word of God in faith and exercise your spiritual authority in Christ Jesus. When you say that you need something, you are only confirming that you don't have whatever it is that you need.

Mark 11:23-24 (KJV) 23 For verily I say unto you, That whosoever shall say unto this mountain, Be thou removed, and be thou cast into the sea; and shall not doubt in his heart, but shall believe that those things which he saith shall come to pass; he shall have whatsoever he saith. **24** Therefore I say unto you, What things soever ye desire, when ye pray, believe that ye receive them, and ye shall have them.

The last verse of this text tells us that we are to believe that we receive when we pray. We don't believe we receive when we physically see the need met. We believe we receive when we pray. If we believe we receive a certain need met when we pray, then we should call that need met, in Jesus' name. If that need was met because you believed you received when you prayed, then that need is no longer a need because it's already been provided. From this point forward, faith will continually praise God for the provision until your faith is turned to sight (when you actually see the provision manifest).

For every Godly need, call, and plan, there is a divine supply to fulfill those needs. Your Father is The Source of the plan. Therefore, He's the supplier or financier of the plan's needs. The Lord doesn't call or ask you to do something without supplying you the resources to get it done. He specializes in asking people to do things when they don't naturally have everything that's needed in order to fulfill whatever it is He asks. The provision follows the plan; the plan doesn't follow the provision.

Sometimes it may seem you have the provision but not the plan. For instance, you may receive a large sum of money unexpectedly and are not immediately aware of its purpose. Money has an assignment in the Kingdom of God, so before you spend a penny, seek the Father's counsel and He will reveal the plan that He has already assigned those funds to accomplish.

Chapter 6

The Present Call of God

If we are going to not only answer but fulfill our Heavenly call, then we must understand the relationship between the pulpit and the pew. If we don't know how these two relate, we are going to end up getting off course and short-selling ourselves when it comes to the fulfillment of our calls in this life. The call is important because eternity matters far more than many truly realize, at least at this stage of things. We must walk worthy of our call.

Ephesians 4:1 (NLT) — 1 Therefore I, a prisoner for serving the Lord, beg you to lead a life worthy of your calling, for you have been called by God.

Many people look at the calling of God on their lives as something that is put on reserve only for the future. We must not fail to realize that we progress in the call of God. Every day of our lives has a call or purpose attached to that day. The call of God is not just something that is put off for us to fulfill in the future, but there is something that we must fulfill in the present. Yes, there is a future call. However, before there is a fulfillment of a future call, there must be a fulfillment of the present call. It's the fulfillment of our present call that enables us to move higher and grow into our future call. In this sense, the call of God is always in the present tense.

In order for the enemy to stop you from fulfilling to the fullness God's future call or plan for your life, he works to hinder you from fulfilling your present call. He works to steal, kill, and destroy what you are called to do presently. If he can successfully stop you in what you are called to do today, he has stopped you from fulfilling your future call. Your present, and how you respond in the fulfillment of the present call of God, is directly connected with your future call.

Lots of people have been sidetracked by the enemy by getting so caught up in looking for the spectacular of the future call that they miss the supernatural in the fulfillment of the present call. You are called to do something presently. You are called to do something right now. As a matter of fact, you are called to do something today. Thank God for all that we may accomplish for the Kingdom in our tomorrows, but let's not forget about what we can and are supposed to do today.

Have you ever thought about what you are called to do to advance the Kingdom of God on the earth today? Be mindful to not overly concern yourself with your future that you miss out on your present. It's our present call that equips and prepares us for our future call.

All of us are servants in the Kingdom of God. We are all soldiers in the army of the Lord. As a soldier in God's wonderful army, where are you called to serve today? How do your Heavenly orders read? Where is your assigned post?

The President of the United States is the commander-in-chief of our armed forces. He issues orders to our troops to do certain things and to mobilize to certain posts or locations all around this world. Most of the time, these orders (or calls to serve) are not delivered to the army privates by a personal phone call or letter directly from his desk with his seal and signature. No, the orders are delivered to the generals that are in command of different branches of service, and those generals issue the order (or call) down the chain of command until it reaches the private level. Then, it is the private's responsibility to respond to the sergeant, or whoever gives them the order, and to obey the instructions of that sergeant.

To disobey a sergeant who has been instructed by his superiors to give a private a certain task or duty to perform, would be the same as disobeying a direct order from the President of the United States because they are all connected. Many times we only look at the President, or leaders close to the heads of various nations, to be the only ones who matter or are important in regards to our duties, responsibilities, or call to service. We forget that there is a chain of command. There is rank and order that must be followed in any branch of the armed services in order for the plan of the commander-in-chief to come to pass.

Also, we need to understand that much training and preparation must take place before one can become an officer in our military forces. One doesn't just join the Navy and next week is promoted to the admiral in charge of the entire Pacific fleet of the U.S. Navy. The United States of America doesn't put novices in positions of great authority. I'm not saying that these people are perfect in all their ways, because you and I know they aren't. However, they do stand in a particular office of authority that must be continually revered, honored, and respected. Always respect the office that the man stands in.

There is a great spiritual parallel here in how the Kingdom of God operates in the earth. Many times our limited view of things is not God's unlimited view of things. Ultimately our calls and assignments begin in Heaven by our commander-in-chief of the army of the Lord. Jesus is our commander-in-chief. He is the captain of the Heavenly hosts. He is the One Who issues calls for service, but many times those calls can seem to come indirectly.

Just as the Army, Navy, Air Force, and Marines are made up of different parts respectively, so is the Kingdom of God. There are different branches of service in the Kingdom of God with different parts and functions (much like a human body, as the Apostle Paul related it).

1 Corinthians 12:12–27 (NLT) — 12 The human body has many parts, but the many parts make up one whole body. So it is with the Body of Christ. **13** Some of us are Jews, some are Gentiles, some are slaves, and some are free. But we have all been baptized into one body by one Spirit, and we all share the same Spirit. **14** Yes, the body has many different parts, not just one part. **15** If the foot says, "I am not a part of the body because I am not a hand," that does not make it any less a part of the body. **16** And if the ear says, "I am not part of the body because I am not an eye," would that make it any less a part of the body? **17** If the whole body were an eye, how would you hear? Or if your whole body were an ear, how would you smell anything? **18** But our bodies have many parts, and God has put each part just where he wants it. **19** How strange a body would be if it had only one part! **20** Yes, there are many parts, but only one body. **21** The eye can never say to the hand, "I don't need you." The head can't say to the feet, "I don't need you." **22** In fact, some parts of the body that seem weakest and least important are actually the most necessary. **23** And the parts we regard as less honorable are those we clothe with the greatest care. So we carefully protect those parts that should not be seen, **24** while the more honorable parts do not require this special care. So God has put the body together such that extra honor and care are given to those parts that have less dignity. **25** This makes for harmony among the members, so that all the members care for each other. **26** If one part suffers, all the parts suffer with it, and if one part is honored, all the parts are glad. **27** All of you together are Christ's body, and each of you is a part of it.

Just as the military force of the United States of America is made up of various officers who are in charge of its command under the direction of the President, so is God's Kingdom and church on the earth. The church of God as a whole, or the entire Body of Christ, is ultimately under the headship of our great shepherd, Jesus. He is the commander-in-chief of it all. However, the church of the living God is also divided up into various branches with different responsibilities in those branches. Jesus, too, has commanding officers or ones that He has put in charge to oversee specific tasks around the world. These officers are important to the smooth running of God's army on the earth. Who are these officers in the army of the Lord?

Ephesians 4:11–13 (AMP) — 11 And His gifts were [varied; He Himself appointed and gave men to us] some to be apostles (special messengers), some prophets (inspired preachers and expounders), some evangelists (preachers of the Gospel, traveling missionaries), some pastors (shepherds of His flock) and teachers. **12** His intention was the perfecting and the full equipping of the saints (His consecrated people), [that they should do] the work of ministering toward building up Christ's body (the church), **13** [That it might develop] until we all attain oneness in the faith and in the comprehension of the [full and accurate] knowledge of the Son of God, that [we might arrive] at really mature manhood (the completeness of personality which is nothing less than the standard height of Christ's own perfection), the measure of the stature of the fullness of the Christ and the completeness found in Him.

The officers in the army of the Lord are as follows: the apostle, prophet, evangelist, pastor, and teacher. Their responsibility is to help lead, guide, and direct the army of the Lord under the leadership of the great captain of the Heavenly hosts, Jesus. This is their call. This is God's plan for their lives. This is their deployment in the earth. These officers are here to help each of us along the way in fulfilling the plan of God on the earth. The Lord can and will speak through these officers as they issue instructions for the church to carry out around the world.

The Kingdom of God is not a democracy where everybody has a vote. It is most definitely a theocracy. What is a theocracy? It is a system of government in which God's officers command the will of God in the earth under the direct leadership of God. This is God's chain of command.

This doesn't mean that the apostle is more important than the Godly businessman who has an assignment to flow billions of dollars into the Kingdom of God on the earth for the gospel. This doesn't mean that this businessman is more important than the apostle, just because he may have more money flowing through his hands. They both have a call. They both have a purpose. They both have an assignment. However, it is of the utmost importance that this wealthy businessman takes his place under the leadership of the one whom the Lord has personally put over his immediate spiritual charge, and that is his pastor.

The call of God for your life is directly connected with the pastor that the Lord has placed over your life. Contrary to popular belief, church members (sheep) really can't choose their pastors (or at least they're not supposed to do so). Likewise, pastors (shepherds) can't choose their sheep. (I've had to dismiss very few people from my church, and when I did it was always the very last resort and it saddened me dearly.) We are all assigned in our respective locations or posts by our commander-in-chief, Jesus, Who is the head of the church.

It baffles me as to why church members sometimes have the idea that they can just pick up and leave a church whenever they don't feel like being a part of that local family (or spiritual post that was assigned to them by God) and choose another post to serve God. I realize that the church isn't the U.S. Navy or Marines, but there's something that can be learned from them in regards to our honor, respect, and submission to their higher purpose or call.

Just think for a moment about things from this perspective. What if your pastor got tired of all your antics, criticism, know-it-all attitude and decided that he was no longer going to show up for service anymore? What if he got out of bed one Sunday morning and decided that he was tired of dealing with all of the griping, complaining, and bad attitudes that have been staring him in the face for service after service and just quit his post? Wouldn't that be wrong? Didn't God call him there? Didn't God issue his Heavenly orders and assign him at that particular post? What if this pastor just went AWOL and didn't even tell his congregation that he was quitting? Wouldn't that be wrong?

Of course that would be wrong, especially to not even show up and quit, but to just leave without saying a word. That would be rebellious to the Lord. That would be blatant insubordination on his part toward the Lord Jesus Christ. Pastors really don't have this luxury that many church members think they have. There is an immediate call that must be fulfilled, even when we don't always feel like it. Even then, we must do it with joy and not allow wrong feelings to get the best of us.

I realize that this chapter may seem a little straight forward, but I believe it's necessary. Sometimes when we are confronted with truth it gets a bit uncomfortable, but it's necessary just the same. There's safety and blessing in truth.

On a personal note, I have been involved in the ministry in one form or another since 1987. My lovely wife, Robyn, has been a part of the ministry all of her natural life up until present day. At the time of this writing, we have seven decades of combined ministry experience. There's been lots of good, and there's been lots of ugly through the years as well. Just when you think you've seen it all from a church member, you see or hear something else that tops the last situation. The Body of Christ is in desperate need of spiritual growth. The church of the Almighty needs much more strengthening and conditioning. The family of God needs to understand the importance of submission to Godly authority. By doing so, the army of God could accomplish so much more in the earth today with their present call.

It's sad to me to hear the stories of pastors and ministry leaders from around the world. They may have different names and faces to their stories in their dealings with their church members, but in essence, they are all the same. It's concerning to me that church members get the idea that they can just pick up and leave because "God told them," and God did it without even consulting His commanding officer who was put in charge of their spiritual well-being, their pastor. This is called insubordination or rebellion. I know these are really strong words, and I truly do realize the seriousness of what I am saying.

Please understand my heart in this matter regarding the present call of God. These are not personal accusations against any particular person, but only the truth being spoken from a heart full of love that desires to see the people of God fulfill their future call. Until God's people have the self-discipline to fulfill their present call, they will never step over into the fullness of all that the Lord has for them in the future.

Chapter 7

Stay at Your Post

Just as I didn't choose my assignment or post as a minister of the gospel, you can't choose yours either. It makes no difference if you are an apostle, prophet, evangelist, pastor, teacher, or a church member who has been sent to assist in the local church. Pastoring a church wasn't my first idea about what I wanted to do for the Lord, but that was God's plan. Pastoring other pastors wasn't my plan, but that was His plan. His plan is far better than my plan could ever be even at its greatest. The Lord places people in the body (His church) as He sees fit. He doesn't place people where it's always comfortable or convenient. Also, He's not a schizophrenic God Who changes His mind from one week to the next because man's personal feelings change.

I realize that posts and assignments change in the Body of Christ from time to time, and I'm all for that, but I also realize that they don't change as often as people think or in the way they sometimes do either.

There is a right way to leave a church family and a wrong way to leave. There is a way that's of God, and then there's a way that's the handiwork of Satan himself.

When the Lord changes somebody's post and assigns different orders, all parties involved will know about these orders, especially the pastor. Orders to change posts don't come wrapped up and delivered through hurt, offense, and blatant rebellion because one refuses to submit to the leadership of his pastor. If your pastor doesn't agree with your decision and the circumstances of your decision, then you are ultimately going against Jesus. Even if you go to another church, get involved, and seem to be perfectly happy with this new church, that doesn't mean that the Spirit of God led you there. Eventually, this rebellion will creep up on you again and history will repeat itself, unless you repent and make amends. How you leave one church is how you enter the next one. It matters far more than people think.

If you leave your pastor and your church for the wrong reasons and without his consent, then you will be beginning the next phase of your church life in the wrong manner. You will enter into another church wrongly and will eventually cause harm there.

Satan is a master deceiver and he will deceive the elect, if given the right opportunity. Many times after people make the decision to leave their pastor and church in a manner that is unbecoming of a Christian, the devil will *honeymoon* them for a while before he launches an all-out assault against their lives to further steal, kill, and destroy.

Don't ever forget that the devil will always give you a *honeymoon phase* at the new church, especially when you left your previous church wrongly. That *honeymoon phase* will eventually come to an end, and then the seeds of discord and rebellion that you sowed previously will come back to produce another harvest. It is very sad to say, but this is spiritual law.

Your present call is directly connected with the post that the Lord has assigned to you, whether that be a pulpit or a pew. Until we fulfill our present call, we can never fully move on to our future call. This is paramount in understanding the plan of God for our lives. The relationship you have with your pastor and your church family is of the utmost importance. Unless something is blatantly going on in a church, such as unrepentant sexual immorality, financial theft, child abuse, etc., you have no business just picking up and leaving your assignment. The Lord places people in church families as He sees fit. He leads them to the pasture where they are to be spiritually fed and equipped to progress in the call of God. It's the devil that tries to pressure people out of their proper post in the plan of God.

Many believers live and die and never fully enter into all that the Lord has for them in their future call because they fail in their present call. Your future call is contingent upon how you handle, respond, and grow in your present call.

Are you fulfilling what you are called to do today? Are you where the Lord called and planted you to be, or did you leave that post because of hurt or offense? Did you leave your post without your pastor's consent? If so, I encourage you to quickly repent of these wrongdoings and your spiritual insubordination by making things right.

In our combined years' experience in the ministry, my wife and I don't personally know of a church member having the love, character, integrity, honesty, and humility to actually do this yet. A highly regarded minister friend that has been around the world and has had decade upon decade in the ministry once told me that he has had this experience and someone came back and repented, but it was only with one person. I haven't seen this yet. However, we are still on the earth and it is most definitely possible. I will remain hopeful, but at the same time, my faith isn't in man but in God.

How do we know when it's time to change posts? How do we know when it's right for us to be transferred under another pastor? How do we know when it's right for a pastor to move on to another post or position in the ministry? These are all important questions that must be covered with much prayer and Godly counsel.

Here's one thing for sure that we must never forget, and this goes from the pulpit to the pew. One reason why many people leave their pastor and church prematurely is because of offense and hurt, which is pretty much the same thing. To leave a church offended because you are hurt at your pastor, or even possibly somebody else in your church family, is completely ungodly. The Lord doesn't lead people out because of an offense, even though there have been multitudes of Christians lie to themselves and others that He has.

This is spiritual immaturity, which can be the result of a weak relationship with the Lord. Don't let this happen to you. For God to lead people in this manner would be totally opposite of God's love and character.

There are many reasons, but honestly, no truly valid excuse for not remaining faithful to your post and the church where the Lord has planted you. Yes, there will be different seasons of emotions that you will experience in your relationship with your pastor and church. The truth is, we are all to be growing in our calls and progressing toward the completion of God's plan for us on the earth. In the process of this, there may seem to be ups and downs. Most people don't remember the good things; they only focus on the things that they *think* are bad.

The present call of God upon our lives must be carefully guarded. One of the ways that we guard this call is to guard it against hurt and offense. Every relationship will be challenged. It doesn't matter who you are, because the devil always comes to divide and separate man from God. The devil will always come to separate you from what God has presently called you to do. He doesn't want you fulfilling the Father's present plan, because then he can hinder you from fulfilling the Father's future plans.

One of the popular phrases that is thrown around so much in churches and conferences around the world is "Dream Big!" I've got no problem with people who dream big, so please don't misunderstand me at all. As a matter of fact, I have big dreams. It's important that *you* have big dreams as well. However, the reality is many of God's people will never fulfill the big dreams until they can fulfill the smaller dreams, and usually, these smaller dreams are deeply intertwined with relationships that the Lord has ordained but the devil destroys.

If the devil wants to attack and hinder the future call of God on your life from coming to pass (the big dreams), then he usually does it by destroying the divine relationships that God has brought in order to help you fulfill those big dreams. There's a lot of hype being preached in the modern church of today such as, "You're special! You can do it! Nobody can stop you! If people don't want to go with you, then you can go by yourself!"

The modern church is very selfish in nature. It really doesn't preach the gospel much anymore because it's too busy preaching something different. It's busy preaching a selfish gospel—the gospel of you, instead of the gospel of the Lord Jesus Christ. This is not okay on any level.

Once again, please hear my heart and don't misunderstand any of this. Yes, you are special. Yes, you are important. I've made that clear in previous chapters of this book. On the other hand, the call of God is not all about you. It's about others. The call of God isn't about making you look good; it's about reaching others. The call of God isn't about self-importance; it's about the importance of remaining humble and being a servant of all. The call of God was never meant to be self-serving, but God-serving.

If you ever view others as a threat to your self-serving ways, then you are falling prey to the devil's trap. If you ever view your church as not serving your needs the way that it should, then maybe something is wrong with you instead of your church. You were sent to that church to help serve and meet the needs of people, not just to focus on your own needs, desires, or wants.

One of the famous lines that is said from disgruntled sheep all over the world in regards to why they left their church is, "I just wasn't getting fed there anymore." Most of the time, these people have come out of great churches that are preaching the pure gospel, and challenging people to spiritual growth and maturity. Usually, if people aren't getting fed anymore, it's because they've stopped eating the food that the church is serving and started eating something that the devil's been serving (which is usually the food of hurt and offense). Instead of causing problems at your church, how about you be a part of the solution to problems at your church? That sounds like a biblical concept to me.

I've said this to people for years, "If you can find a church where you can get better spiritual food than what I've been serving you, then you need to go there because I want you to have the best." As long as a pastor preaches and teaches what the Lord has instructed him to minister, the food will always be fresh and delicious.

Sometimes I may serve meat and potatoes, other times it may simply be a nice salad. Not everybody likes vegetables, but we must have them in order to live a healthy life. I even like to serve my church a little cake, cookies, and ice cream from time to time. However, I realize that we can't live on that every service. We must have a well-balanced diet. Not everything I minister will tickle the ears; sometimes it will prick the heart. Personally, I'd rather hear messages that don't try to hype me up and tickle my ears by telling me what I want to hear, but rather what I need to hear that pricks my heart. This is where we will find true spiritual growth because then we are then eating true spiritual food that nourishes our souls.

Ecclesiastes 10:4 (AMP) — 4 If the temper of the ruler rises up against you, do not leave your place [or show a resisting spirit]; for gentleness and calmness prevent or put a stop to great offenses.

I love this verse here in Ecclesiastes 10:4. Even if someone I love and respect slips and gets angry with me for no reason at all, I must not leave my post. I must not allow offense to come in and the devil to drive me out. Ministry leaders aren't perfect people. They are people who are growing just like you are, even though they may have a different position of responsibility in the Body of Christ. Sometimes the leaders who are used on the front lines the most are the ones who seem a little rough around the edges. Many times this is all part of their equipping in regards to their call.

I remember years ago when I first went into the ministry and began to get introduced to many of God's generals, I used to think they were hard core and sometimes a bit insensitive toward others. These people lead major ministries that have literally shaken this world with the gospel. Then as I began to mature in Christ and got to know many of them on a personal level, I soon began to realize that they weren't mean and insensitive, but they were quite the opposite. They were very much loving and sensitive people. They loved God and me enough to tell me the truth, regardless of my feelings. Negative feelings are nothing more than the voice of our flesh. They are the voice of our *unrenewed* or *unsubmitted* minds. I don't always need people to tell me that I'm doing something right. What I do need is for somebody to point out something which I'm doing wrong that I should change, and then begin to do it properly.

Hebrews 13:17 (NLT) — 17 Obey your spiritual leaders, and do what they say. Their work is to watch over your souls, and they are accountable to God. Give them reason to do this with joy and not with sorrow. That would certainly not be for your benefit.

If the Lord ever wants to change your post in the Body of Christ, He will not only speak to you, but He will also speak to the ones He's placed you under. You are under their spiritual leadership and oversight so that they can help watch out for your souls. If you sense a change coming and the Lord moving you in another direction, then very humbly and kindly speak with your pastors and ask them to pray with you. Don't ever go to your pastors with a decision regarding leaving their ministry and covering having your mind already made up. The wise man will always include their counsel. The humble man will always ask them to pray and seek God with them. The Godly man will not leave if his pastors give him a different counsel. He will trust God to speak and allow it to come to pass in its perfect timing. If it's God today, then it will be God tomorrow. If you believe the Lord is leading you in another direction, then your pastors will know it as well and release you with their blessing.

Pastors must stand before God and give an account for your soul. As long as we have loving and truthful pastors, despite how people respond, the pastor will never be in trouble with God. However, there are many sheep that have put themselves in trouble with God because of their wrong behavior in leaving a church. Just as shepherds will have to give an account unto God for their part, their sheep will also have to give an account before God regarding their humility and submission to the will of God.

I realize, once again, that this is pretty strong, but I believe it's necessary. It's time that the truth be told. I'm not talking about ungodly pastors who are controlling and manipulating people's lives. As a pastor, I have enough trouble controlling my own life, and I sure don't want to control anybody else. However, I also know I have a responsibility to not only submit to the will of God, but also be truthful in all my dealings with His people. I'm talking to you about spiritual things not natural things.

As a pastor, I never tell people who they should or should not marry. I never tell people where and when to go to work. I never try to get too involved in too many personal decisions that people have to make, especially financially. Many times people will come and ask me my thoughts, and sometimes I share them, but sometimes I don't (depending on the situation). However, I always direct people to the Lord and His Word. I always point people toward the will and plan of God. If it's promoting the plan of God, then I will always be for it. If it's not promoting the plan of God, then I usually try to let them know in a nice way. Sometimes, I don't say anything at all because I know that it won't be received. The latter has happened a multitude of times throughout the years, but I always endeavor to be there whenever help is needed and to point people to freedom and the light.

Here's how you can know if someone leaves a church with the pastor's consent, particularly if this person is or has been in leadership. The pastor will announce the change well in advance of the person's leaving, and then they will lay hands on him in his final service and bless him before sending him on his way. Also, when a former church leader (or even member for that matter) leaves his church correctly, there will always be an open line of communication even after his departure. In other words, there will never be any hard feelings, slander in social media, etc., and whenever this former church member is ever seen, he will always be greeted with open arms and a very warm heart filled with nothing but genuine love. The Lord never just cuts anything off all at once. As a matter of fact, rarely does He ever cut anything completely off at all. There should always be some type of connection.

In smaller congregations, it usually doesn't matter if a person leaving is in leadership or not. Then, as a church family you can still lay hands on the ones moving or leaving and send them forth with your blessing. You can't always do this in larger congregations, but smaller ones will do this when only a few hundred people may be involved.

The Lord will always place you under whom and what you need in order to fulfill what He's called you to do in the earth, no matter how big or insignificant you might think it to be. He connects people as He sees fit. He establishes and ordains the relationships you will need in order to succeed in your tour of duty. Protect these relationships at all costs because the devil will always try to put these relationships to the test. Know and understand how the pulpit and the pew relate. Let's pass these tests and put the devil on the run. Let's fulfill what we are called to do today so that this world can experience much better tomorrows.

Always be honorable to those whom the Lord places you under. Always be respectful to their face and especially behind their back when they aren't around. Always speak highly of them and never put them down by questioning their decisions or leadership (you may not know everything involved that led them to make a particular decision). Don't second guess their love for you. Always know they are looking out for your best interest and not their own.

Refuse to allow discouragement to enter into your thinking. Realize that you progress in the call or plan of God. You never start out where you end up and you never end up where you start out (or at least you shouldn't). It's a divine progression that comes to pass as we begin to develop in our relationship with the Lord of our call. I believe the hand of God is on your life and that the Spirit of God is directing your steps.

Chapter 8

Engraved by God

Fulfillment of the call to God and for God is of the upmost importance. It matters that we answer the Father's divine call to a relationship with the King of the universe. It also matters that we answer the call to do whatever it is the Lord has assigned us to do in the earth.

God most definitely doesn't call the qualified, but He does expect the called to eventually become qualified to fulfill His call. The qualification process isn't always your schooling or degrees. There are many people with college degrees (even in theology) who aren't yet fully equipped to fulfill the call of God upon their lives because they haven't yet let the Holy Spirit work in them like He so desires.

I want you to notice something very important here that the Apostle Paul states in the beginning of his letter to the church in Philippi. Please take special note of what he said in verse 6 and verse 11.

Philippians 1:3–11 (NLT) — 3 Every time I think of you, I give thanks to my God. **4** Whenever I pray, I make my requests for all of you with joy, **5** for you have been my partners in spreading the Good News about Christ from the time you first heard it until now. **6** And I am certain that God, who began the good work within you, will continue his work until it is finally finished on the day when Christ Jesus returns. **7** So it is right that I should feel as I do about all of you, for you have a special place in my heart. You share with me the special favor of God, both in my imprisonment and in defending and confirming the truth of the Good News. **8** God knows how much I love you and long for you with the tender compassion of Christ Jesus. **9** I pray that your love will overflow more and more, and that you will keep on growing in knowledge and understanding. **10** For I want you to understand what really matters, so that you may live pure and blameless lives until the day of Christ's return. **11** May you always be filled with the fruit of your salvation—the righteous character produced in your life by Jesus Christ—for this will bring much glory and praise to God.

The Father is continually working on the inside of us through the power of His Holy Spirit. There is a good work of God that is going on at this very moment on the inside of every Christian. This inner working of the Holy Spirit is something that is crucial in order for us to be able to fulfill the plan of God for our lives. This work within us is something that will continue until we are face to face with the Master. As long as you are here on this planet, the Holy Spirit will continue this work within.

You are most definitely a work in progress and still under construction at this very moment. There are many things that must be constructed on the inside of each of us that will qualify us in our ministry for the Lord. Jesus is the Master carpenter and is a specialist at building and rebuilding lives.

This work within is the process of building character. The construction project that the Holy Spirit is overseeing is the formation of character in our souls. Most earthly building projects have a projected end date. Usually, man can build a house within a six month period of time. Skyscrapers can sometimes take years and years to build because it's a bigger project. The bigger and more complex the project, the longer it takes. The taller the building, the more work that is required in order for that building to stand tall and not topple over during a windstorm or earthquake. Regardless, there's always an end in sight when the construction process nears its completion.

In regards to the inner working of the Holy Spirit in our souls (our minds, wills, and emotions), this is a life-long endeavor. No matter what your natural age is, or even how long you've been a Christian, you are a perpetual building project while you are here on the earth. The primary construction and building that the Holy Spirit works and does in His people is the forming of Godly character.

Matthew 5:48 (AMP) — 48 You, therefore, must be perfect [growing into complete maturity of godliness in mind and character, having reached the proper height of virtue and integrity], as your heavenly Father is perfect.

We all know that you and I are far from perfect. We've all used that excuse to try to cover our shortcomings along life's journey. However, Jesus said that we must be perfect, and then He went on to describe the perfecting (or maturing) process. He said that we must be growing into complete maturity of godliness (which means to be like God) in mind and character by reaching the proper height of virtue and integrity, just as our Heavenly Father is perfect.

This construction project that the Holy Spirit oversees is the total and complete transformation of our souls (our minds, wills, and emotions) to be aligned with His. It is the rebuilding of character in a soul that has the tendency to not always want to do what is right. The construction of character in your soul is a necessary ingredient in order for you to fully accomplish and fulfill the call of God that's upon your life.

What is character? What is this trait that the Holy Spirit is perpetually developing within us? Our English word **character** comes from the Greek word *kharakter*, which means *an engraved mark, symbol, or imprint upon the soul*. It means *to engrave with a pointed stake by scraping and scratching*.

Sometimes people purchase gifts for others and then have them engraved with either their initials or their names. Sometimes they're pens, and sometimes they're jewelry. However, the best example for understanding engraving is to look at a tombstone that's used to mark someone's grave after that person has passed away. Tombstones are just exactly that—they are made of stone. In order for the stone to be engraved with the deceased's name, birthdate, and passing date, there is a lot of scraping and scratching that's required because granite can be very hard. I realize that rocks don't have feelings, but if they did, I'm sure that this would not be a very comfortable process to undergo.

This inner working of the Holy Spirit that each of us experience on a daily basis is the engraving of character upon our souls. There's a lot of scraping and scratching that transpires on the inside of minds, wills, and emotions until character is truly formed, constructed, or engraved deep within us. Sometimes the engraving process happens and we feel very little in the process, while other times the pain is very real and sometimes seemingly unbearable.

This word character later became known as *the sum of qualities that defines a person.* In other words, *it is the mental and moral qualities that make up a man or woman.*

Remember, Paul said in Philippians 1:11 that we should always be filled with the fruit of our salvation, and the fruit of our salvation is the righteous character on the inside of each and every believer.

Philippians 1:11 (NLT) — 11 May you always be filled with the fruit of your salvation—the righteous character produced in your life by Jesus Christ—for this will bring much glory and praise to God.

The fruit of our salvation, or being born-again, is a righteous character. I don't know about you, but I really want to be filled with the fruit my salvation. I want to be filled with the righteous character of God on the inside of me. What about you?

When and just exactly how is the Holy Spirit able to build Godly character on the inside of us? How is character developed? How is it grown? How is it engraved? The Holy Scripture gives us this answer.

Romans 5:3–5 (AMP) — **3** Moreover [let us also be full of joy now!] let us exult and triumph in our troubles and rejoice in our sufferings, <u>knowing that pressure</u> and <u>affliction</u> and <u>hardship</u> produce patient and unswerving endurance. **4** <u>And endurance (fortitude) develops maturity of character</u> (approved faith and tried integrity). <u>And character [of this sort] produces [the habit of] joyful and confident hope of eternal salvation</u>. **5** Such hope never disappoints or deludes or shames us, for God's love has been poured out in our hearts through the Holy Spirit Who has been given to us.

Construction time is a time when things are sawn in two. Pieces of wood are cut off and removed that aren't necessary because they are too long, too rough, or not shaped properly. Construction is the time when nails are sometimes driven and glue is sometimes used to hold various pieces of the construction project together.

The pressures, afflictions, and hardships that we face in this life come to everybody, and it's in the enduring of these pressures, afflictions, and hardships that we will have the character of God formed within us. The pressures of this life aren't always fun, but they are most definitely there. Hardships are just exactly that, they are hard times, but it's in these pressures and hard times that the Lord is able to work His engraving process in our souls. The tests and trials that we may experience in this life are what will eventually build us into the people that God has ultimately called us to be. This is the equipping we need in order to fulfill the call of God.

In light of all this, we must also realize that God is not the author of pain, sickness, disease, or poverty on any level. He's not the author of the bad things that happen to us in life such as rapes, failed relationships, or even bad business deals. However, we must note that Jesus is the Master Redeemer and He doesn't waste anything. He is a specialist in taking something the devil meant for our destruction and turning it around so that we benefit somehow or some way in the process. God will use negative events that happen in our lives which have the potential to leave us completely devastated and without hope, to ultimately build strength of character within our souls. He redeems these events and causes character to be engraved within us and for us to come out stronger than we've ever been before.

If you want to fulfill the call of God for your life, then Godly character is a requirement. Character is what will bring you out of hardships and sufferings. Character is what will cause you to not fail under pressure. Character is what will position you for a promotion beyond your wildest hopes and dreams. Character is what will be the necessary ingredient that will bring your BIG DREAMS to pass. This is why we must make every effort to allow the Holy Spirit to build the character of God on the inside of us, because the fulfillment of the call of God will be the result.

Chapter 9

The Character and Love Connection

Once Godly character begins to build on the inside of you, this character is what will see you through to victory in all your tomorrows. Character in the challenges you face today is what will promise you a far better tomorrow.

Let's read our scriptures in Romans once again, and this time, I want you to take notice of what verse five says.

Romans 5:3–5 (AMP) — **3** Moreover [let us also be full of joy now!] let us exult and triumph in our troubles and rejoice in our sufferings, knowing that pressure and affliction and hardship produce patient and unswerving endurance. **4** And endurance (fortitude) develops maturity of character (approved faith and tried integrity). And character [of this sort] produces [the habit of] joyful and confident hope of eternal salvation. **5** Such hope never disappoints or deludes or shames us, <u>for God's love has been poured out in our hearts through the Holy Spirit</u> Who has been given to us.

It's interesting to see the connection here between the pressures, afflictions, and hardships of this life with the love of God. Love is the foundational character that the Holy Spirit is engraving and imprinting in our souls by lots and lots of scraping and scratching (uncomfortable times).

Love is of the utmost importance in our day and age. Letting love lead and guide our lives is a must. Living by love is a lifestyle that we must all adopt. It is the character-refining process that the Holy Spirit is working within us as Christians in order for us to fulfill the call of God. Love empowers us to fulfill the plan of God. Without love, the plan of God will go unfulfilled, and we will have to stand before God's throne and give an account for our actions (or lack thereof).

Luke 14:25–30 (NLT) — **25** A large crowd was following Jesus. He turned around and said to them, **26** "If you want to be my disciple, you must hate everyone else by comparison—your father and mother, wife and children, brothers and sisters—yes, even your own life. Otherwise, you cannot be my disciple. **27** And if you do not carry your own cross and follow me, you cannot be my disciple. **28** "But don't begin until you count the cost. For who would begin construction of a building without first calculating the cost to see if there is enough money to finish it? **29** Otherwise, you might complete only the foundation before running out of money, and then everyone would laugh at you.

30 They would say, 'There's the person who started that building and couldn't afford to finish it!'

Love isn't real love unless it costs you something along the way. Walking in love is the cost of being a follower of Jesus Christ. It is the cost of discipleship (being like Jesus). We must count or consider the cost of being a disciple of Jesus because it requires us to not love others more than we love God.

When Jesus said that you must hate your father, mother, wife, children, brothers, and sisters (and even your own life), He was referring to you having a lesser degree of love for them than you have for God. In other words, God must always be first before everybody else. Never put your family before your relationship with the Lord. By learning to manage your time wisely, this will help you live wholeheartedly for God and your family will not suffer in the process. Actually, it will be quite the contrary. They will be blessed because of it.

I understand that sometimes people will have to make sacrifices with their time in order to fulfill the call of God. However, I also know that God always makes up for it in one way or another. The fulfillment of the call of God on your life will not leave your family suffering, if it's done properly. You need your spouse and your spouse needs you. You need your children and your children need their parents. The Holy Spirit will never lead you away from your family, but will allow you to be closer to your family when Jesus is first. He will always help you keep things in balance. Remember, if you are a parent, you aren't just raising a child, but you're raising another one who is called.

Loving others is a decision. It's not a feeling. Have you ever noticed that when you decide to walk in love toward others, it seems as if all hell breaks loose in that relationship? The devil will always challenge your decision to walk in love by waging a spiritual battle against your decision.

Jesus has already stripped the devil of his authority and power. As far as Jesus is concerned, the devil has been whipped. However, we still have to contend with his ridiculous antics here in the earth from time to time. The spiritual battles that we face are mostly within (within our thinking). The battle is waged between your ears. This is where the enemy will attack your decision to walk in love (in your thinking).

Every relationship will be challenged from time to time, no matter who you are, and in this challenge you have to make the decision to always walk in love toward the other party. The devil will always challenge you. It's in this challenge that character is built in your heart.

Far too many of God's people fail in their relationships because they aren't aware of how to win these spiritual battles and that's by remaining to walk in love. Always look at spiritual battles as an opportunity for you to develop strength of character (or the image of Christ being engraved upon your soul through all the bumps and scrapes along the way). Always use spiritual warfare as an opportunity to develop character. When Satan finally realizes that his attacks against you are only making you stronger, he will cease in his maneuvers against you. Defeat only occurs when you give Satan access to your life by not walking in love.

1 John 3:14 (NLT) — 14 If we love our Christian brothers and sisters, it proves that we have passed from death to life. But a person who has no love is still dead.

It proves that you are born-again and the character of God is being built on the inside of you when you love others. Absolutely nothing will work in your life without the character of God begin formed within you. Love never fails.

Have you ever noticed that fruit immediately begins to spoil once it is detached from the vine? The love of God is the root to the life of God and all that is associated with this divine life (health, healing, prosperity, etc.). When you stop walking in love, you will begin to operate in selfishness and the good fruit of God that you desire to enjoy will spoil in the process.

Not walking in love will eventually affect your physical health. It will also affect you financially. Why? It's because you will be weak in character and won't be able to withstand the devil's attacks against your life. A characterless life will be a life void of the power and authority of God. It's a Godly character that will enable you to walk in your spiritual position of authority and power over the works of Satan in the earth. Without the character of God being engraved upon your soul, life will be difficult.

Motives are everything. Let everything you do in this life be motivated only by love. Let the love of God always be your standard and guide. Let the love of God influence your decisions instead of being pressured to make a wrong decision. Character is what will sustain any relationship. Character is what will sustain you during times of misunderstandings. Character matters. It will sustain you in hardship. It will sustain you in any adversity. Character is what will see you through to victory when other people's relationships crash and burn and have their fruit spoiled in the process because they disconnect from the root of life.

Character is the decision to do the right thing in any given situation. Character is the decision you make to do what is right when you are tempted to do what is wrong. It makes no difference how much you try to convince yourself and others that wrong is right. Wrong will always be wrong and that's not a Godly character. Whenever you feel pressured to make a wrong decision, even though you know the proper response, take time to allow the character of God to build on the inside of you and don't succumb to the attack of the devil against your mind.

The choices that you make in this life will determine whether or not you are developing the character of God. What kind of decision you make under pressure determines whether or not the character of God is being engraved deeper upon your soul. The choices you make today in the heat of the battle will determine whether or not you fulfill the call of God upon your life. Don't let the devil pressure you out of fulfilling the call of God—both the call to God and for Him.

You will never rise above the character of God that is being formed within you. The deeper character is engraved upon your soul, the higher you will rise.

As a pastor, I've encountered lots of people along the way who have had good intentions, but their character was very shallow, and consequently, those intentions were left unfulfilled. When a person's intentions and actions are opposite of each other, you must examine this person's character. Many have good intentions, but their actions end up pulling them in a different direction whenever the pressure is on.

Why do people choose to act differently from what they know is right (their intentions)? Very simply, they aren't willing to undergo the pain of their souls being engraved (scraped and scratched). They aren't willing to humble themselves and have the character of God constructed on the inside of them. The cost is too great for them to pay. The love of God isn't as important as they once thought, so their selfish nature causes them to seek their own bitter and ungodly ways.

The soil of our lives matters more than anything. The seed of the Word and love of God are continually being sown into our lives, but we choose what type of soil these seeds are sown in. In Mark's gospel, we find the very famous parable of the sower. In this parable Jesus explains the four types of soil where the seed of the Word of God is sown. In order to bring clarity to the subject we are discussing at the moment, I want us to read this passage from the Message Bible (which is a paraphrase). I want you to particularly notice the type of soil mentioned in verse 17.

Mark 4:13–20 (The Message) — 13 He continued, "Do you see how this story works? All my stories work this way. **14** "The farmer plants the Word. **15** Some people are like the seed that falls on the hardened soil of the road. No sooner do they hear the Word than Satan snatches away what has been planted in them. **16** "And some are like the seed that lands in the gravel. When they first hear the Word, they respond with great enthusiasm. **17** But there is such <u>shallow soil of character</u> that <u>when the emotions wear off and some difficulty arrives, there is nothing to show for it.</u> **18** "The seed cast in the weeds represents the ones who hear the kingdom news **19** but are overwhelmed with worries about all the things they have to do and all the things they want to get. The stress strangles what they heard, and nothing comes of it. **20** "But the seed planted in the good earth represents those who hear the Word, embrace it, and produce a harvest beyond their wildest dreams."

Character isn't always what you say or your good intentions, but it is the actions that take place after the words and intentions have been uttered. Don't let your actions be contrary to your words or intentions. When you do, then you are choosing to not have the character of God formed within you during this season of trial and testing. The fulfillment of the call of God matters. Character is what will qualify you in the fulfillment of the Father's plan.

How one responds or acts reveals his character. Intentions don't reveal character, and words don't even reveal character. They can be small indicators, but the real disclosure of character can only be found in our actions.

Proverbs 20:11 (The Living Bible) — 11 The character of even a child can be known by the way he acts—whether what he does is pure and right.

Actions reveal motives. Actions reveal our commitment to the love of God. Actions reveal our strength or weakness of character. Let's make sure that we allow the good work that the Lord has started inside of us move forward by making the right decisions when the pressure is on to make the wrong decisions.

It's only natural to want to find the quickest way out of the fire when the heat is on, but sometimes the quickest way out of the fire is to remain in it and allow it to burn up everything in our souls that doesn't belong there in the first place. Once again, God is not the author of hurt and pain, but sometimes in this life we all must endure a little pain in order to ultimately experience comfort.

Having the love and character of God formed within us is part of the preparation process of fulfilling our earthly assignment given to us from Heaven. Every day you are being prepared for a better tomorrow. It is character that will only produce lasting fruit in your life—both in this life, as well as the life to come. Character is what will sustain the ultimate fulfillment of God's call and fuel you to run your race and win.

Yes, you are called. Yes, you're still a work in progress and still under construction. Yes, you will probably make a few mistakes along the way, but a Godly character will always pull you back on track and the Lord will help you retake and ultimately pass the failed tests. Yes, you are growing in your relationship and call to God, and in the process, you will be empowered by His divine grace in your earthly work for the Lord.

You are called to Him and for Him. Now, it's time to fulfill that call.

Are you ready for a change?

Jesus wants more than anything else to have a relationship with you on a personal level. Having a relationship with the King of Kings and the Lord of Lords is not about empty dead religion—it's life in all its fullness. If you are ready for a real and lasting change in your life, then it is time to turn your life over to Jesus and make Him your Lord. He'll not only save you from spending an eternity in Hell, He'll heal your broken body, He'll heal you emotionally, and He'll even bless you financially as you begin to put Him first in your life.

Salvation is a free gift that has been made available to everyone who will receive it. Heaven is a very real place, just like Earth is a very real place. The only way for you to enter Heaven is for you to believe on the Lord Jesus Christ, confess Jesus as Lord with your mouth, and allow Him to take up residence inside your heart.

Romans 10:9 (The Message Bible) *Say the welcoming word to God—"Jesus is my Master"—embracing, body and soul, God's work of doing in us* *what he did in raising Jesus from the dead. That's it. You're not "doing" anything; you're simply calling out to God, trusting him to do it for you. That's salvation.*

The very first step in receiving Jesus as your Lord is to admit that you are a sinner. The Bible tells us in Romans 3:23 *"for all have sinned and fall short of the glory of God."*

Secondly, you must believe in your heart that Jesus died and paid the ultimate sacrifice for your sins, was resurrected from the dead three days later by God the Father, and now sits at His Father's right hand in Heaven interceding for you to God. You must know and realize that Jesus is your only answer and He alone provides you access to this place we all call Heaven. If you're ready to begin a new life and want a fresh start, pray this prayer out loud from your heart.

Dear God, I know that I have fallen short in many areas of my life and sinned. I now make the decision to make Jesus my Lord and Savior. Jesus, I want to thank You for dying on the Cross for me and for paying the ultimate price for my sin. I acknowledge that You are the Son of God and that You are the way, the truth, and the life. I invite You, Lord Jesus, to come and make my heart Your home. I receive my salvation by faith, and I thank You, Lord, that I am now born-again and a resident of the Kingdom of God. In Jesus' name, amen.

Now what?

One of the ways that we develop a relationship with the Lord is by reading His Word, the Bible. There are many easy to understand translations that are available at your local bookstore. Some of the translations that I recommend are: the New Living Translation, the New International Version, the Message Bible, and also the Amplified Bible. Any one of these would be a good place for you to get to know the Lord in a better way. The Bible is actually comprised of 66 books, and a good place for you to start studying is the gospels (Matthew, Mark, Luke, and John).

Now that you are born-again, it is highly important for your spiritual growth and maturity that you get plugged in to a Bible-believing, Bible-teaching church that will show you how to live by faith and experience victory in every area of your life. It does matter where you go to church because not all churches are the same. It does matter who your pastor is, because not all pastors are the same. Ask the Lord to show you where you need to go to get the help that He wants you to have. Ask the Lord to lead you to a good pastor that will help you grow and become the person that God wants you to be.

Congratulations! You're on your way to experiencing the goodness of God in your life. God is a good God and He longs to share His goodness with you. The Lord loves you so very much and He will continually demonstrate that love in and through your life in the days ahead. God desires that you live a happy, healthy, and wealthy life. As you follow Him and learn more of His Word, all these things belong to you as a Christian. Once again, congratulations! Something good has just happened to you!

To invite Wayne Hancock to speak for your church or conference, or for a complete list of ministry resources and other books by Wayne Hancock, please contact:

Wayne Hancock Ministries
420 N. Wakea Avenue
Kahului, Maui, HI 96732
(808) 244-4992
Email: info@waynehancock.org

Internet: www.waynehancock.org

www.ingramcontent.com/pod-product-compliance
Ingram Content Group UK Ltd.
Pitfield, Milton Keynes, MK11 3LW, UK
UKHW041944230426
12048UKWH00008B/135